Peggy
Summer 77

HOW TO BUILD, MAINTAIN & ENJOY YOUR OWN
HOT TUBS
LEON ELDER

**Photography by Sam Dabney,
Tim Crawford, Wayne McCall
Cartoons by Bruce MacDougall**

**VINTAGE ✸ BOOKS
A Division of Random House, Inc.**

VINTAGE BOOKS EDITION May 1975
Copyright © 1973, 1975 by Capra Press
Published in the United States by Random House, Inc., New York,
and simultaneously in Canada by Random House of Canada Limited, Toronto.
Originally published in another version by Capra Press, in 1973.
Library of Congress Cataloging in Publication Data

Hot tubs.
1. Baths.   2. Bathing customs.   I. Title.
TH6493.Y68   643'.55   74-30046
ISBN 0-394-71324-9

Manufactured in the United States of America
First Edition

Grateful acknowledgments to: Walker A. Tompkins, Santa
Barbara *News-Press* historian, for permission to reprint his article
"Hot Springs, 1988"; Richard Johnston for permission to
reproduce his "Physical/Emotional Satisfaction Scale" on page
39; Bruce MacDougall for his various cartoons; Frank Frost for
his construction diagrams on pages 47 & 48; George Christians
for author's photo on page 77; Gretel Ehrlich for the coil photo
on page 31; Hokusai (eighteenth century) for his print on page 9;
Don Lothe for his graph help; Patty Henry for the assembly
diagrams on pages 25 & 26; George Beronius for his chapter
"Hot Tubs and Sex"; Richard Fish for photographs on pages
49 & 88; tub builders Gary Gordon and Richard Grant; Steve
Wright for the photographs on pages 75 and 81; and to the
enthusiasm of hot tub owners, builders and soakers such as Fred
Carr, Eric Cassier, Patty Bruce, Lynn & Wendy Forman, Heidi,
the Knolls, the Sanders, the Peakes, the Johnstons, the Dabneys,
the Palmers, Pat McGinnis, Richard Petersen, John Smith, the McCalls,
the de Milles, Tim Crawford, Vic Kondra, the Don Timms, Dr.
Lawrence Williams, Psychiatrist H. Neil Karp, Kerry and Tony
Tomlinson, Linda Harwood, Kathy Koury, Judy & Molly Young,
and others too coy to be mentioned.

Cover photograph by Zachary Franks.
Used by permission of Tony Seiniger Associates, Los Angeles.

The best time is at night, in windy rain, an old oak groaning and creaking overhead. Naked and shivering, you stare at the steaming pool and put one foot in. The stinging tells you it's being cooked, yet other people are in up to their chins, laughing and beckoning. The cold rain encourages you in the cauldron. A searing line slowly rises to your chin and you don't dare move. Then within five minutes you feel melted and happy, even into your bones. Someone passes a glass of wine. Pelted by rain, it bubbles like champagne. Fifteen minutes later you rise into the wind—it feels delicious. Now you understand how the Finns can run naked from a sauna to hurl themselves into the snow. You sink easily back into the water again and gaze at the nude people, some standing in halos of steam, others hunched down to their chins. They all appear curiously pleased with themselves, & you think—what bliss!

**Dedicated to
warmth, trust & camaraderie
in an overcrowded
& suspicious world.**

CONTENTS

THE ORIGIN OF HOT WATER AND THE DESCENT OF MAN INTO IT

Darwin, had he expanded his interests, might well have made an interesting study of the evolution of the hot tub. Since he didn't, I'll give it a try.

It's easy to guess that early man, and conceivably even his primate forerunners, must have found pleasure in thermal springs. While one brother was diligently inventing the wheel, another was probably lolling in a sulfur pool. Whether he actually lured others in to join him, to make it a communal affair, is lost in some dim recess of clouded history.

But we do know that early civilizations—the Egyptians, Babylonians, Romans, Greeks, Turks, Finns, Hawaiians, American Indians and the ingenious Japanese all invented some forms of group bathing. The award for size goes to the Romans—their colossal tiled *thermae* could accommodate up to 18,000 bathers simultaneously. American Plains Indians built sweat lodges—arched huts on stick frames insulated with a mixture of mud, pine needles and grass, and sometimes covered with buffalo hides. Steam was created by pouring water on hot rocks in a fire pit inside the lodge. These lodges were usually placed close to a stream or lake so a good steaming could be followed by a cold water bath. This same humid-steam principle was applied by the Turks in the famous bathing establishments of Islam; the Finns, on the other hand, preferred the dry heat of the *sauna.* But wherever they were, whether they accommodated a handful of American Indians or thousands of Romans, the baths became social centers, places of conviviality and relaxation where a person could go for fun or for therapy, to exchange the news of the day or to expel evil spirits from the body. In tribal life, refusing to bathe with a friend was considered an insult.

With the decline of the Roman Empire, bathing fell into disfavor in Western society. King John of England is said to have bathed only every three weeks. King Henry IV formed the Order of the Bath in order to assure that his knights would bathe at least once in their lifetime—during the dubbing ceremony.

Where is everyone?

Queen Isabella of Spain, Columbus' mentor, boasted that she'd had only two baths in her life—one at her birth and the other at her marriage. In the seventeenth century bathing made a comeback of sorts, at least among the nobility, and lords and ladies often entertained visitors while in their baths. Having one's portrait painted in the bath was considered chic.

The popularity of bathing ebbed and flowed with the centuries. In colonial America the Puritans scorned soap and water. Bathing was a dirty word—it was injurious to health, promoted nudity and encouraged promiscuity. In some states it was actually illegal to bathe. But in 1796 a Dr. Samuel Thompson of New England used steam bathing to successfully treat his daughter for an ailment that other physicians were unable to cure. Dr. Thompson had discovered the secret of the healing powers of hot water that for centuries has attracted people to the spas and *Baden* of Europe. Nevertheless, the bath didn't really become a fixture of American society until the presidency of Millard Fillmore, when the first fixed bathtub was installed in the White House. By the 1870's the hot water heater was introduced to American homes, and the cast-iron bathtub, resting on its lion claws, was followed by the overhead shower. The shower is a typically American invention—something to hop into, soap and rinse, then towel off and be on your way.

While Americans were making their bathing quicker and more efficient, across the world in Japan people for centuries have been soaking for *relaxation,* in the company of family and friends. The *ofuro,* an indoor tub usually made of teak (a richly beautiful wood containing natural oils that make it impervious to water), is standard equipment in many Japanese homes. Before dinner, the family and their guests will soap and rinse themselves outside the tub (The Japanese get clean in order to bathe, while Westerners bathe in order to get clean!), then loll in their *ofuro* in water temperatures up to 115 degrees. Those

Japanese families who can't afford tubs of their own use the public baths (*sento*), where for the equivalent of twenty cents they can soak for hours with friends of both sexes, gossip, and discuss the news of the day. In Japan, public coed nudity is not considered sexually provocative—a potentially revolutionary notion that we in America are discovering with the growing popularity of communal tubs and free beaches.

So if we are looking for the direct ancestor of our hot tub, it must be the Japanese *ofuro*. We think of the Japanese as ingenious imitators, producing their versions of everything from shoehorns to automobiles in copycat profusion. But here's a case where we may have imitated them!

In a curious turnabout, last spring a two-man team from the Tokyo Broadcasting Company arrived in Santa Barbara, California, to film a television documentary on the phenomenon of the hot tub. We were curious to see how they would react to our somewhat boisterous translation of their ancient and venerable rite of bathing.

"This woods, you carr—ah—*led* wood?" the interviewer asked, delicately touching the tub as if it were made of rice paper.

"Redwood," I answered, "from northern California."

"Hmmm. Is velly ord? More ord than teak?"

Satisfied that it was indeed properly venerable, our interviewer turned his back while twelve of us undressed and climbed into the redwood tub. We were happy and laughing together while he furiously took notes in Japanese calligraphy.

Meanwhile, the cameraman, with his shoulder-mounted Bolex, had managed to climb high into an oak tree for a bird's-eye view. That first shooting session took an hour, the Bolex whirring almost continuously, recording the antics of carefree, wine-drinking Caucasians in their outdoor *ofuro*. We urged the crew to take a break from their work and join us, but the journalist asked for a "lainwater check," and laughed uproariously. At one point he dunked a hand into the water and told us the temperature was enjoyable. "Onry the Samurai rike it more hot," he said. "They boil themserves."

The Japanese spent two days with us. We took them to a variety of hot tubs—on hilltops, in canyons, in housing tracts, on ranches—and they seemed

genuinely awed that there were so many of them. But it seemed impossible to determine what they *really* thought of the American hot tub until the last shooting session in the afternoon of the second day. That's when the cameraman, after exhausting his last cartridge of film, reverently laid down his camera, took off his clothes, bowed nakedly to the West, streaked across the deck and swiftly lowered himself into the steaming water.

"This!" he exclaimed. "This is *it!*"

It seems natural that Santa Barbara should be the spiritual home of the hot tub. The canyons above the city have been known for their natural hot springs since ages back when they were the property of the Indians. It was only a matter of time until this great natural resource was discovered and "developed" by the newcomers to California—as Walker Tompkins attests.

HOT SPRINGS, 1888

By Walker A. Tompkins

When Wilbur Curtiss came to Santa Barbara in 1854 he was suffering from an incurable disease which doctors told him would end his life within six months. (Why doctors always granted a doomed patient six months more of life is as much a mystery as finding a cure for the common cold.)

Mr. Curtiss accepted his prognosis philosophically, but was determined to see as much of Santa Barbara's scenic wonders as time and strength permitted. Thus, during the course of a hike in the Montecito foothills, he encountered an old Indian bathing in Hot Springs Creek.

An Indian youth who accompanied Curtiss on his walks around the countryside indicated that this husky oldster was past his hundred and tenth birthday, and that he attributed his longevity to bathing in some hot springs which gushed from the cliffs farther up the canyon.

Wilbur Curtiss was curious to see these health-giving springs. A few hours' climb up the creek brought him to Montecito Hot Springs, which had been a popular bathing spa for soldiers of the Stevenson Regiment when they occupied Mexican Santa Barbara in 1847-48.

There were four springs. The water, heated to 116 degrees, contained sulfur, arsenic, iron, magnesium and other health-giving minerals.

Not having anything better to do, Curtiss soaked himself in the warm waters. He even drank from one of the sulfur springs. And a miracle happened: his health began to improve. Six years later, when he obtained a homestead in Hot Springs Canyon which included the spa, Curtiss was a picture of vibrant health, and indeed lived to a ripe old age.

The fame of Curtiss' springs spread afar, and by the 1880's, when Santa Barbara became a popular watering place for elite health seekers who had previously given their patronage to Baden-Baden, Spa, Aix-la-Chapelle or the thermal springs in Italy, the Montecito Hot Springs were a very valuable status symbol indeed.

In the late 1880's a three-galleried wooden hotel was built on a bench above the springs, as shown in the above rare picture from the past, reproduced from a stereoscope slide of 1888.

Curtiss' homestead became the property of a stock company composed of wealthy individuals who furnished the Hot Springs Hotel with priceless antiques, Oriental rugs and *objets d'art*. Mrs. Martin Kimberley, widow of the noted sea captain and cofounder of Trinity Episcopal Church in 1869, was hired to operate the resort, which was open only to the upper crust of society.

After the turn of the century, the Hot Springs Hotel became even more exclusive; anyone with a bank account under seven digits needed not apply.

In 1920 a disastrous forest fire cleaned out Montecito Hot Springs Canyon and leveled the hotel. It was rebuilt in 1923 under the ownership of a corporation limited to seventeen members, all Montecito estate owners, who also controlled the Montecito Water Company.

H. B. Jones was the resident custodian of the new Hot Springs Hotel until it too was destroyed in the Coyote Fire of 1964. It was his job to have baths ready for patrons who would telephone in advance of their arrival by limousine.

Today, a mile-and-a-quarter hike up a private dirt road from the end of Hot Springs Road brings one to the site of the old luxury spa. Although not open to the public, the mineral springs still flow as they did when the aborigines partook of their curative waters. There is even talk that a third, and hopefully fireproof, hotel will rise someday on the sandstone foundations of the old.

There has been some mild controversy over the origin of the American hot tub—who put the first one together, when and where. We could give the credit to an obscure renaissance man named Kyburz, as Mountain Driver Dick Johnston does, or to Ed Stiles of Marin County, or to a summering romantic on Martha's Vineyard. But the version of the legend that appeals most to me, for its authenticity and color, comes from Will Henry and his witnesses. If this account suffers from provincialism, know too that it's true.

THE FIRST HOT TUB ON MOUNTAIN DRIVE

It is said that the first hot tub was observed in its native habitat in the foothills behind Santa Barbara on the night of the vernal equinox, back in nineteen aught and fifty-eight. It was a fine redwood tub steaming in the rain at the bottom of Will Henry's land, a short stroll down a dirt path from his adobe house. In the early evening the tub stood unnoticed. Sounds of merriment and the music of recorder, concertina and pump organ leaked from the windows during lulls in the lashing storm. The Mountain Drivers were having a banquet. An observer would have seen them in their most outlandish finery—gowns of theater-curtain velvet, old graduation formals, Victorian dresses and sequined shimmies from the twenties. One man in tails with a bemedaled sash across his chest might have been a Bulgarian count. Another man wore a wine-stained scoutmaster uniform. Next to him sat a crony in a canvas safari suit with a pith helmet that must have been nailed to his head—it never came off. Bobby Hyde, father-founder of this postwar community, lounged in his GI camouflage jump suit.

A book should be written about the Mountain Drivers, the phenomenon that they were. Call them a disparate group of young settlers who had no common ground except land. Or think of them as utopians struggling together for freedom and self-expression. The scene began at the end of World War II when Bobby Hyde, a visionary approaching fifty who had spent a quarter-century building stone houses, writing books and playing Go, bought a hundred acres of steep chaparral land behind Santa Barbara. A dirt road called Mountain Drive bisected this land. Bobby built his house on a prime saddle that looked down over the city to the harbor and the Channel Islands beyond. He planted olives and avocados around his house and encouraged young couples to build on his land, which he sold by the acre, fifty dollars down and fifty a month. This made it possible for most of the new settlers to have enough money left over to buy cement, nails, window glass and pipe. Hyde let them use his cement mixer and gave them instruction on building walls of rammed earth, adobe or stone. He showed them the usefulness of old materials—railroad ties, telephone poles and freight-car stakes, all virtually free in those days. He also showed them how to relax after a day's labor by loading them into his weapons carrier and driving them to the Las Cruces hot springs, in the hills forty miles away.

Will Henry was one of these early Mountain Drivers. Most were artists, writers and craftsmen. One was a mechanic and salesman who specialized in keeping fifty-dollar cars running. Another was a specialist in old washing machines and water heaters.

This group was not harmoniously communal. They had no common belief, no credo, no organization. Many weren't even on speaking terms. But in spite of themselves they *were,* in the eyes of outsiders, a Group. As a group they either originated or perpetuated a number of ideas and institutions that are still part of the Santa Barbara scene: the Midsummer's play and frolic, the Bobby Burns haggis banquet, the Grape Stomp, the Twelfth Night celebration, the philosophical Sunset Club, annual Pot Wars, and their mimeo paper, *The Grapevine.* They invented the car-stake module, using seven-foot timbers whose original purpose had been to hold cargo onto railroad flatcars and were sold cheap or thrown away after the cargo was delivered. They painted the word WHOA on county stop signs marking boundaries to their domain.

Many of their inventions and rituals had meaning only to them. But the one notable product of their ingenuity, one that spread like a small contagion beyond their world to be accepted enthusiastically elsewhere, was the homemade hot tub.

Henry and friends used much ingenuity to make that first hot tub. Their makeshift water-heating system used diesel oil dripping into a stove pipe with a vacuum cleaner turned backwards for a blower. Firebrick stacked around coiled copper tubing provided a heating chamber. Somehow it worked. The tub itself was the same redwood vat used *every year* for the Grape Stomp and out of which thousands of gallons of Kinevan Red had been bottled. Strange that, for all their inventiveness, the Mountain Drivers had never before conceived of using it as a hot tub. For years they had thought nothing of piling into Bobby's weapons carrier and driving two hours over mountain roads for a soak in Big Caliente or Las Cruces. Sheer torture it had always been, following a long hot soak, with bodies soft and complacent, every nerve at peace begging for sleep, to dress and take a long jouncing ride home

With the backyard hot tub that ordeal was eliminated. In the years to come, as hot tubs began to proliferate, a prime principle was to place the tub as close to the bedroom as possible. After a soak the body craves bed.

On that historic night, after the last lamb shank was licked clean, the Mountain Drivers stood and shed their garb around the table, using the chairs as clothes racks. The overdressed became undressed. Ladies with back zippers were obliged by the nearest gentleman. After a few minutes of contorting, everyone became his original self. "Welcome back, everybody!" exclaimed Peggy, shedding her Victorian dress. She plucked the tiara from her coifed hair, yanked out some strategic pins and let her hair tumble down over her bare shoulders. Will put on Handel's *Water Music,* and the company scampered out into the rain, down the short path to where the hot tub awaited them.

One by one they lowered themselves in, ah, so gingerly. Soon enough they became comfortable, their heads in a ring resting against the redwood planks. They raised their glasses and toasted the "miraculous waters."

"Back in Baden-Baden," the erstwhile Bulgarian count began, "I bathed with cripples. The curative powers of that water were remarkable. One old geezer had to be wheeled to the bath and lifted in. Yet, after an hour's soak, he literally danced away under his own power. In my notes at home, I think I have an analysis of that water. Now if we could just import dehydrated packets . . ."

"It's *all* right here!" cried Peggy. She climbed out of the tub, pranced over to a verdant bank and snatched up the spring's first canyon sunflowers and some sprigs of mint. By throwing them into the water, she became the first person to use additives in a Mountain Drive hot tub. "All ye of crippled humor and insomnia are hereby cured," she declared.

Whether they knew it then or not, a new life dimension was in the making. Bobby, the visionary, suggested rustling up more tubs and spotting them all over town so no one would ever be more than a mile away from one.

"Yep, hot tubs are here to stay," mused Will Henry.

Some years later Henry inaugurated his Hot Tub Catering Service for the underprivileged. On the back of his dilapidated truck, "Lupita," a Chevy one-tonner he brought back from Ensenada, he carried a redwood tub and a butane heating system.

Since that historic night, a great number and variety of hot tubs have appeared both inside and outside the native habitat of Santa Barbara's Mountain Drive. This book illustrates and describes some of the working tubs of Santa Barbara. Its emphasis will be on the homemade hot tub, the do-it-yourself job that requires only some ingenuity, romantic drive, work and a few dollars. There is at least one commercial, packaged hot tub on the market (see page 64), not to mention the super-chic and super-expensive jacuzzis installed by some swimming pool contractors, but these by and large are beyond the scope of this endeavor.

Hot tubs bring peace. As Chaucer wrote: "His herte bathid in a bath of blisse."

THE
WOODEN
TUB

The most common hot tubs are wooden tanks, four to six feet in diameter. Although new ones are available, most of those seen in the Santa Barbara area are old and have been transplanted from farms or wineries. They are usually redwood, although some oak and even pine tubs have been seen. A redwood tank, set up properly, will last a lifetime or two. The fact that it has already spent fifty years storing farm water or fermenting grape juice has done little to shorten its life expectancy. Its very history is appealing to tub owners, who take care to display whatever legend may have been stenciled on the side: "No Fishing," "Fermenter Vat No. 2," "Cap. 536 Gals." These tubs are deserving of respect. In this day of baroque, paisley and spray-gun art, the hot tub stands stately and unadorned. The only alterations that most owners can bring themselves to make are sculptural. Since most tubs come too tall, they have to be cut down, either all the way around or with a section or two cut away for entries. Getting into some gives you the feeling of boarding a boat.

For those of you who are not used to dealing with cubic figures it might be surprising to learn that a five-foot tub filled with three and a half feet of water is holding 515 gallons, while a six-footer holds 742 gallons. If you have reason to be concerned about the amount of water or fuel for heating you use, this can be a consideration. Also note that while a five-foot tub will accommodate eight snuggling people (with a heroic ninth in the middle), a six-footer will hold thirteen. The weight, which shouldn't matter if you are set up outdoors on firm ground, is two tons for a five-footer and three tons for the six-footer.

FINDING A TUB

Scour the nearby countryside for the sight of an old water tank, usually on stilts, that seems abandoned. If he no longer uses it, the farmer might let you have it for the taking; it's just an eyesore to him. If you don't have a crane or enough helpers to move it bodily, get yourself a can of Liquid Wrench, a heavy crescent wrench and a bright crayon. Be sure to number all the staves in sequence before dismantling. They are *not* identical. All the staves are slightly beveled, and some have been hewn to fit between their neighbors. In a sense, what you are doing is the equivalent of taking apart a hand-fitted boat. The floor planking, too, should be keyed to show where each plank fits into grooves near the ends of the staves.

The barrel hoops surely will be rusted. Several inches of thread will protrude through each nut. With liberal dosings of Liquid Wrench, a wrench and muscle, you should be able to persuade the hoops to open—like bracelets. It's a good idea to number the hoops as well and even to mark where on the thread the nut was cinched up to.

If you find no water tank on a farm, try a winery. Many are converting from wood to stainless steel these days and might be willing to sell you an old fermenter. Check the smaller wineries. The big operators seem only to have tubs the size of rooms.

If nothing turns up at a farm or winery, you can build your own tub or buy a new one from a cooper. If you do elect to build a tub, a square or rectangular shape is advisable. A round one takes special skill. Only people with the tools and know-how of Fred Carr, builder of the automated oval tub, should undertake such a project.

For the record, mention should be made of prefab fiberglass tanks. These come from Hollywood, naturally, and cost more than wood. And they don't feel loving.

A good cooper and dealer in both new and used tanks is Alex McCollom of San Jose, California. In New York City, redwood or cedar tubs of any size can be ordered from the Rosenwach Tank Company. In Santa Barbara the tubs are being built by Gary Gordan and Richard Grant, 433 North Quarontina Street.

INSTALLING IT

Clear a fairly level area as close to your bedroom as possible, since a deep relaxed sleep is the natural aftermath of a good soak. Whether you have bought a new, disassembled tub from a cooper or have acquired an old water or wine tank, the procedure is the same. The floorboards will rest on two or three chime joists (four-by-fours are sturdy enough), and these joists can be laid on concrete foundation piers, a poured slab, or directly on a bed of coarse gravel if you have good drainage. (Figure 1) The piers can be bought precast at lumberyards for about a dollar apiece. Level them with a generous puddle of concrete.

Now lay the chime joists parallel and centered, keeping in mind that they must be cut to fit *inside* the staves and support *only the floor of the tub.* Tanks are designed for the hoops to contain the water. If the weight were taken by the stave ends, the structure would be violated and the grooves that receive the bottom planking would twist or crack. Use a long level and shim the joists if necessary.

Assemble the bottom boards. Start at the center, using dowels to lock the pieces together. (Figure 2) It's a good idea to butter the edges with roofing mastic, particularly if the tank is an old one. Be sure to lay the bottom boards at *right angles* to the joists. Tap them lightly together, then tack two laths across them to hold them in position during assembly. (Figure 3) Use small nails that will *not* go through the boards. Do *not* nail the bottom boards to the joists. Now apply mastic to the outer edge of the bottom boards all the way around.

If you have a key stave, predrilled with thru-wall fittings, position it facing toward the pump, and see that it spans a joint between two bottom boards. (Figure 4) Using a sledge and a block of scrap wood (so not to scar the staves), tap the stave halfway on. Let it lean outward slightly. If it seems loose and doesn't hold, brace it with a piece of lath.

Now set the rest of the staves, tapping each halfway onto the bottom boards, but tightly against its neighbors at the bottom. (Figure 5) Let all of them lean outward slightly. New tanks usually have four or five staves marked by the cooper giving hoop position. These should be spaced at roughly equal intervals. A tip: have your helper stand on the floorboards to keep them from shifting while you tap on each stave from the outside.

24

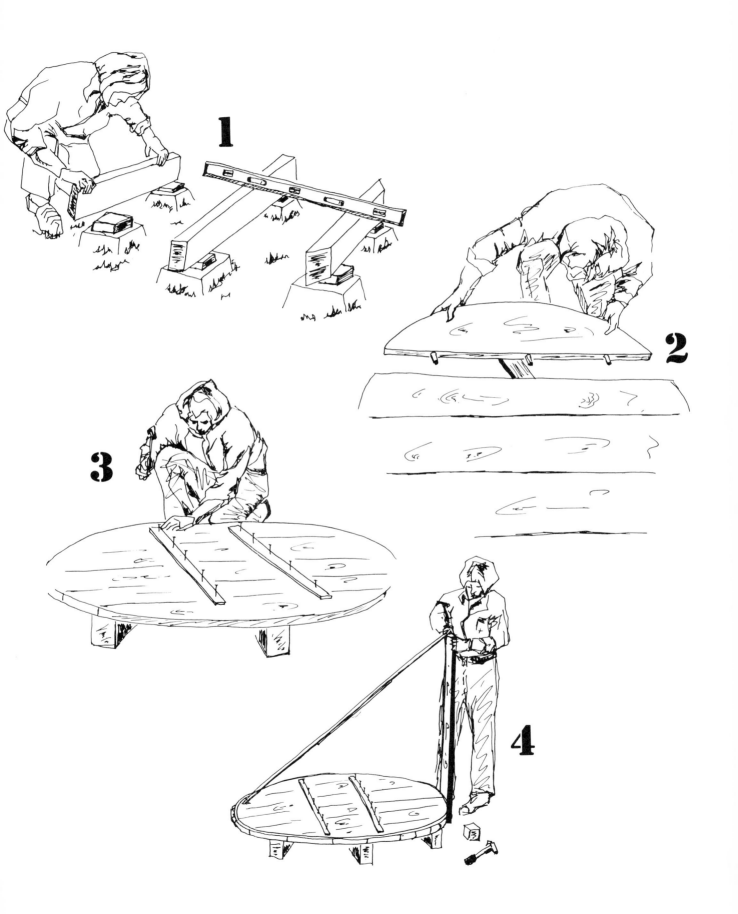

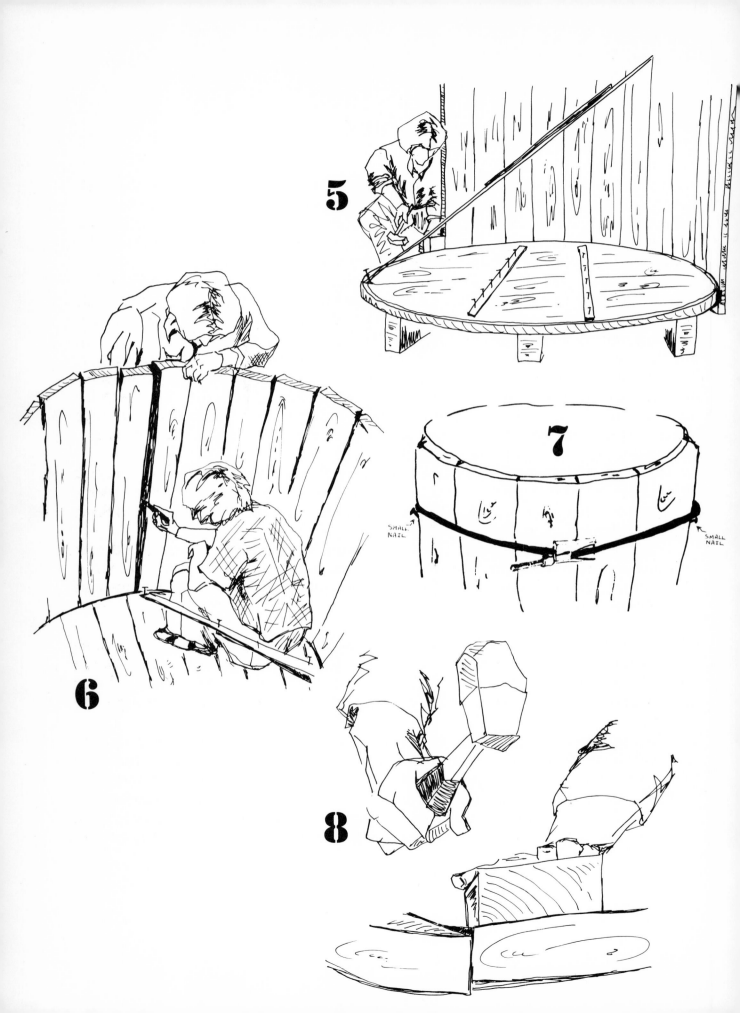

5

6

7

SMALL
NAIL

SMALL
NAIL

8

If you have a new tub, the last stave must be cut to width. This is the only cutting necessary. Mark the width accurately from the inside, at the bottom. (Figure 6) Any lumberyard or home craftsman with a table saw can cut this for you. It's important that this last stave be cut on the same bevel as the others. If it is cut slightly oversize, a hand plane can be used to correct this.

At this point you may find that your partner is trapped inside. Help him or her out with a sky hook or stepladder. Before putting on the hoop, drive small nails into the marked staves (if there are any) about one-fourth inch below the spacing marks. These nails will support the hoops until they are tightened. Slip on the lowest hoop first with the threaded end to the left. Put the nut on and take up most of the slack, but do not tighten. The center of the lug should span the joint between two staves. (Figure 7) The remaining hoops should each be spaced equally around the circumference to the right from the one below, lugs *always* spanning two staves. Spacing is not critical as long as tension is distributed fairly evenly around the tank.

When all the hoops are in place, tighten each lug evenly and lightly, starting at the bottom. At this point any inside bracing should be removed. Using a block of wood and hammer or sledge to round out the tank and force the staves flush on the inside. (Figure 8)

Solid blows on the bottom hoop will drive it slightly into the wood and seat the staves onto the bottom boards. Tighten lug and repeat the operation two or three times. Then repeat for remaining hoops working upwards. Now lugs can be tightened securely.

Now that the tub is assembled, install your bench planks about eighteen inches from the bottom. A pair of two-by-tens cut to conform to the curve are wide enough. Support with a leg near each end and attach with glued dowels or brass angle fittings. Be sure any screws or holes don't go all the way through the staves.

Now you've cinched up the hoops; everything looks tight. You fill your new tub with water from the garden hose, and to your horror, it sprouts a hundred leaks. Like a new wooden boat, your tub won't hold water well right away. Be patient. As the hours pass the wood will swell and the leaks will disappear. In fact, rather than filling your tub immediately, a better plan is to hook up a sprinkler and let it spray the wood for a few hours, even overnight. A good tub will swell and become watertight without caulking. But some older tubs that have suffered the ravages of weather, weevils and woodpeckers may need caulking, particularly when you can see daylight through some joints. Boat shops have a good new plastic putty that can be applied to wet surfaces. As a final resort, if the tub seems too far gone even for caulking, you can glass it like a surfboard, with resin and matt cloth. The only real objection to this is aesthetic. Most hot tub purists don't like the feel of plastic and insist that wood is the only compatible material to lean against.

Once your tub is filled it should always have some water left in to keep it tight. A glassed tub, however, can be emptied and left to dry.

Now that you've got the tub holding water, your next step is to drill two holes—a high inlet just below water level, about 42 inches above the floor, and an outlet at the bottom. The best fitting for this job is a bronze through-hull that boat chandleries carry. These come in different sizes. A three-quarter or one-inch size is recommended for most systems. The fittings are expensive, however (approximately ten dollars each), and many tub owners have simply pounded rigid pipe through a tight hole which has been doped with silicone mastic. If a slight leak develops it will provide a humid environment for any mint or ferns you might plant around the base of the tub.

The tub now needs a cover or lid, something light and easily removable that will keep out leaves and dirt and hold in the heat. Wood is favored for its insulating qualities, even something as thin as quarter-inch plywood reinforced by a couple of one-by-two ribs to prevent warping. Another possibility is a canvas tonneau that snaps around the edges. Keep your tub covered when not in use, to guard against children as well as small wild creatures such as lizards, mice and frogs.

So now there she sits, the noble tub, tight with water and waiting to be heated.

HEATERS

You have, say, 500 gallons of cool water and you must bring it up to at least 105 degrees. Since there's no practical way of doing this in one pass (the average household heater holds about 30 gallons of water), you must recirculate the water through a heating system many times before it will be hot enough. If you begin with water at 60 degrees, this process can take from two to sixteen hours, depending upon the kind of heater you have.

If gas is handy there are many cheap, even free, types of heaters available. The most common, though the least efficient, is the familiar household tank heater. Junkyards are full of them. Often there is no more wrong with these than a small leak, and you can often get one for the asking. You are operating a low-pressure system, and the tank probably won't leak at all with your hookup. Set your heater so the top is fairly close to the water level of the tub. Take a line from the drain outlet of your tub (here it's a good idea to put in a tee with a hose bib facing straight out so you can irrigate your trees or garden with used tub water) to the bottom drain nipple of the heater. Cap off the cold water pipe on top of the heater, then run a line from the hot water side to the tub's inlet. This simple plumbing can be done with galvanized, copper, schedule 40 plastic pipe or heavy-duty appliance hose like the kind used in washing machines. Plastic pipe is the cheapest and easiest to work with, and it has good insulating qualities. It will cut down heat loss many times over metal pipe. Its only drawback is its tendency to sag, so it should be supported in spans over two feet.

If it's a tank heater you must have, remember that a small twenty-galloner will heat as quickly as a larger one and be less conspicuous. But your circulating water will be heating at only two or three degrees an hour.

A much better heater is the coil type enclosed in a cast-iron casing. A gas burner on the bottom heats coiled copper tubing and is twice as efficient as the tank heater. Fifty years ago these household "side-arm" heaters were common. Watch the junkyards for them. They show up sometimes from old demolished houses. They will heat your water four or five degrees an hour.

29

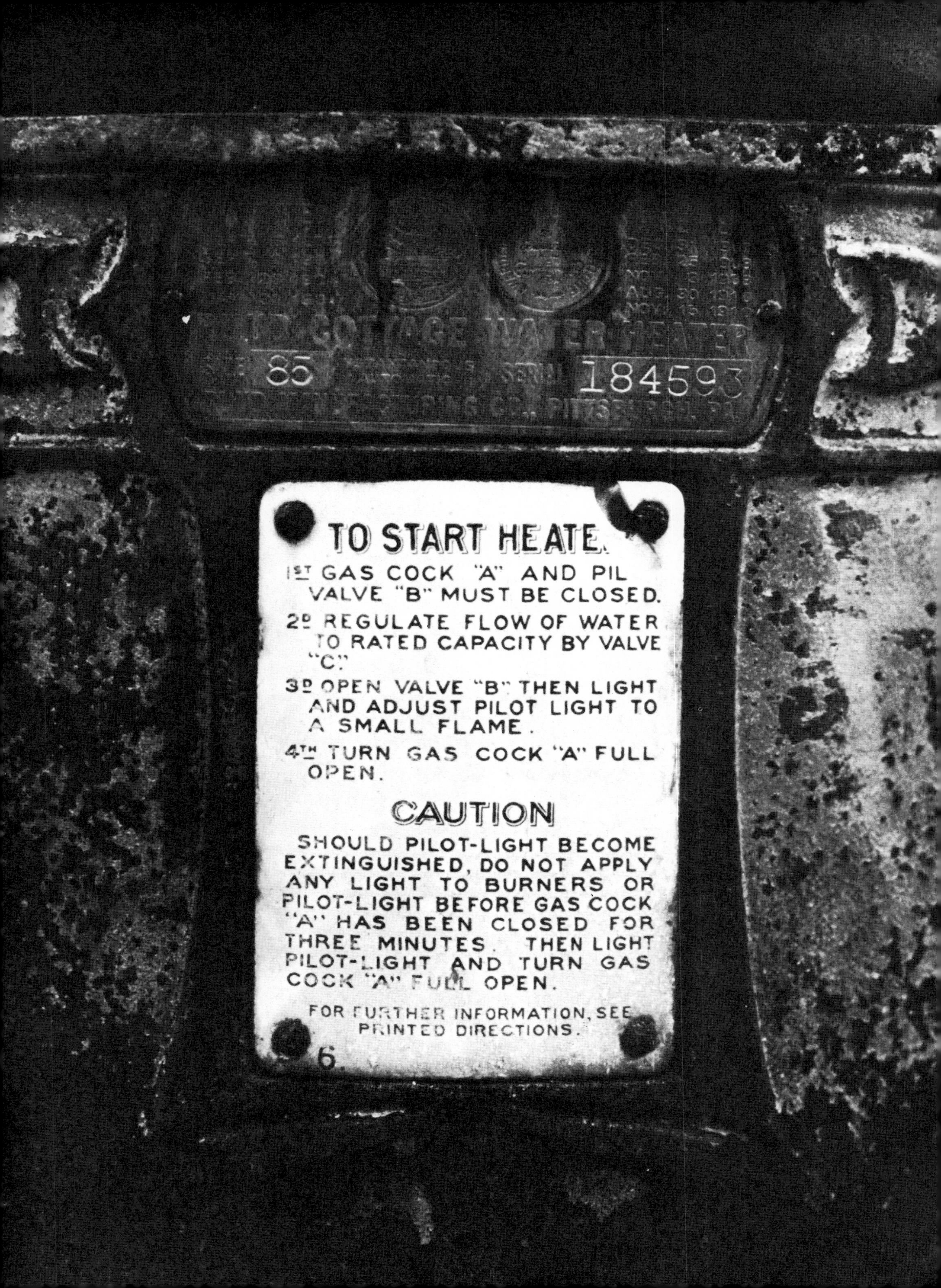

TO START HEATE

1ST GAS COCK "A" AND PIL
VALVE "B" MUST BE CLOSED.

2D REGULATE FLOW OF WATER
TO RATED CAPACITY BY VALVE
"C."

3D OPEN VALVE "B" THEN LIGHT
AND ADJUST PILOT LIGHT TO
A SMALL FLAME.

4TH TURN GAS COCK "A" FULL
OPEN.

CAUTION

SHOULD PILOT-LIGHT BECOME
EXTINGUISHED, DO NOT APPLY
ANY LIGHT TO BURNERS OR
PILOT-LIGHT BEFORE GAS COCK
"A" HAS BEEN CLOSED FOR
THREE MINUTES. THEN LIGHT
PILOT-LIGHT AND TURN GAS
COCK "A" FULL OPEN.

FOR FURTHER INFORMATION, SEE
PRINTED DIRECTIONS.

6

COTTAGE WATER HEATER
85   SERIAL 184593
PITTSBURGH, PA

For superfast heating, twenty-five degrees an hour, snoop around for a "flash" heater like a Ruud Model 100. These are used by laundromats, car washes, hotels and many institutions. The disadvantages are you'll need a bigger gas line—one inch instead of a half-inch—and these monsters roar when they're fired up. But to heat a thousand gallons of water in an hour or so is spectacular. You can be completely spontaneous and have almost an instant hot tub soak if the right people unexpectedly show up on the horizon. If one of these super heaters doesn't appear in a junkyard, check with your local swimming pool equipment company.

If natural gas isn't available, you can use portable butane tanks. Then there are kerosene, oil and electric heaters, although the latter is usually ruled out as too expensive. The army has developed an immersible kerosene heater that can keep garbage cans of dishwater piping hot. Though we've never seen one in a hot tub, it's conceivable it would do the job. But the fumes wouldn't be pleasant and it would have to be removed to make room for people. As a last resort, build a wood or coal fire directly under a system of copper coils.

Some ecological advantages to wood-firing??

PUMPS

Since the water must be kept circulating through the system, a pump is necessary. Simple convection will work, but slowly, and it makes the system susceptible to vapor lock if the water is heated too fast. You don't really need much of a pump unless you have a big flash heater or install a filter. You need only enough pump to keep the heating water moving. There is nothing to gain by circulating vast amounts of water through a relatively slow heater. Look for old washing-machine pumps, bilge pumps, booster pumps, swimming-pool or garden-fountain pumps. Most of these have built-in motors; some are submersible; others require a small external motor. In any case, ground the line from the pump and motor back to the house ground. Sears sells a ground fault circuit interrupter that gives protection from electrical leaks too small to trip a circuit breaker, but strong enough to be dangerous.

The pump should be mounted low, between the tub outlet and the heater, so it will keep its prime. It should be accessible for periodic cleaning and oiling and should be shielded from the weather by a box. Some pumps are noisy. Noise can be reduced by mounting the pump on a rubber pad and using rubber hose connections to the pipe.

Be sure to screen the outlet hole inside the tub to keep foreign matter, such as berries, leaves and jewelry, out of the system. Use copper, aluminum or brass screen, of course.

Always turn the pump on before lighting the heater; otherwise you could be faced with a steamy blow-out a while later. Keep those hundreds of gallons of water nicely flowing when the heater is on. When the water is hot enough, turn the heater down or off. At night when the lid is off and people in, the tub water temperature will drop rather quickly unless you keep the burners at simmer.

FILTERS

Most Mountain Drive tubs don't have filters, though that means changing the water every day or two. Since most of the owners have thirsty orchards or vegetable crops, it's no concern. The installation of a good filter means that you should rarely need to change water. But it is another expense and something else to take care of. Swimming-pool contractors and supply houses seem to be the best source of filters. A common type is a diatomaceous earth disc filter rated for 10,000-gallon capacity. Circulate water through the filter at least two hours a day and flush out filter bags every week. There is also a paper cone filter system. Pump and filter come in a single unit, selling new for about twenty dollars. The cone filter units, however, are fairly expensive and need replacement about twice a month.

The best filter of all, the nonmedia Tubmaster, is described in "The Anatomy of the HOTUB" on page 67. Similar filters can be bought at pool supply stores.

If you do install a filter, you might as well add an automatic timer and a thermostat that uses 24 volts from a step-down transformer. That will give you a deluxe hot tub system offering you a good soak at any hour, day or night. A dial setting and it's done. This is optional, of course. Most Mountain Drive tubs aren't used more than once a week or so. The hot tub soak is considered an Event. The scrubbing, filling and actual lighting of the heater is part of the Ritual.

ADDITIVES

Since used wine tanks are usually very acid, neutralize your first tubful of water with soda ash. You can buy a pH kit for approximately four dollars. It is desirable to maintain the pH at 7 to 7.4 to give the most life to chlorine. Michael Peake recommends pouring five or six glugs of liquid chlorine around the water's perimeter each day. Then too, if you have a filter system it's good to "shock" the tank every six weeks with a half-gallon of chlorine. Add swimming pool acid (cyanic acid) if the water becomes too alkaline.

The faint chlorine smell is unfortunate, but can be disguised in many ways. This can be left to your own invention, but noteworthy additives that followed Peggy's bouquet of mint have been jasmine blossoms, oil of wintergreen, sassafras, essence of orange, sage, patchouli oil and any of the spa mineral salts on the market. The latter smell authentic, if not good. Anyone laved with suntan oil should be asked to shower first. It is highly polluting.

For diversion, Mountain Drivers have on occasion added floating balloons, flotillas of wind-up toy boats, rubber ducks, bubble bath, floating candles and even a portable underwater bubble hose that gave everyone the jollies one zany moonlit night.

LIGHTING

This subject confronts us with delicately differing schools of thought. One school calls for the very dimmest of lighting, presumably because there are features best hidden, or because in darkness there is more freedom to cuddle. The other school wants ample light so as to admire the sight of their happy nude friends. It seems best to have your lighting flexible to suit the temper of the soakers. In any case, lighting should be soft, like that produced by candles and lanterns. One of the more festive tub scenes is lit by Christmas tree lights strung in an overhead tree. Many tub sessions are in daylight, illuminated by the smiling sun.

Ed Stiles, the innovative hot tub designer from northern California, has installed underwater lighting for a client who feared "dark waters." He started with marine portholes, and adapted them as needed.

TEMPERATURES

This is a matter of dispute, controversy and personal tolerance. People's thresholds vary greatly. A delicate newcomer may withdraw a timorous foot from 104° water exclaiming, "Owww, it's *scalding!*" A seasoned Japanese *ofuro* soaker will find anything under 120° too cool. We find the most congenial temperature for Westerners is 106°. At that temperature you can soak comfortably for an hour, occasionally sitting up on the edge for a cool airing, and receive the full benefits of thermal relaxation. But if you want the heat to penetrate your bones, try 110° to 112°. You won't stay in as long, but it brings deeper satisfaction. As a rule then, 106° is best for socializing, while 110° is most therapeutic. Buy a good underwater thermometer and use it. A few degrees makes a great difference. At least two hot tub owners have their thermometers wired to electronic dials mounted indoors so they can keep a close eye on temperature.

One of the most experienced hot tub owners, Dick Johnston, having observed over the years a correlation between temperature and the behavior of his guests, became inspired to research the phenomenon. He embraced the findings of Kyburz (ca. 1200 B.C.), legendary inventor of hot water, added his own observations and devised "The Johnston-Kyburz Physical/Emotional Satisfaction Scale," which he consented to have reproduced.

38

THE JOHNSTON-KYBURZ PHYSICAL/EMOTIONAL SATISFACTION SCALE

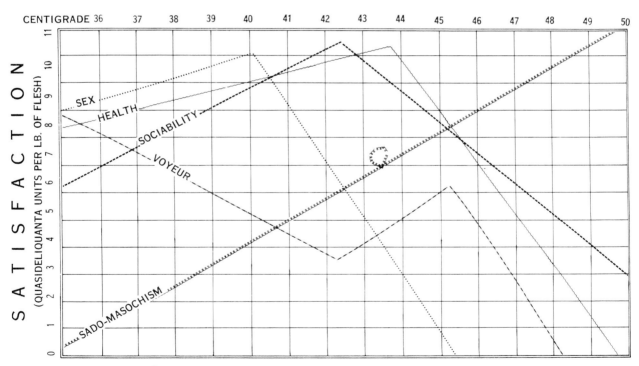

CENTIGRADE 36 37 38 39 40 41 42 43 44 45 46 47 48 49 50

S A T I S F A C T I O N (QUASIDELIQUANTA UNITS PER LB. OF FLESH)

11 10 9 8 7 6 5 4 3 2 1 0

SEX

HEALTH

SOCIABILITY

VOYEUR

SADO-MASOCHISM

TO CONVERT CENTIGRADE TO FAHRENHEIT: MULTIPLY BY NINE, DIVIDE BY FIVE, ADD THIRTY-TWO

AMENITIES

Provide pegs for towels and clothes near the tub, a bench or log to sit on while removing footgear, a hammock or two to dream in after a soak, and a ring of narrow shelves around the tub for wine cups. Most tub owners forbid glass in the tub area and furnish plastic or paper cups. Broken glass underwater is nearly impossible to see. In parts of Hawaii a small one-man barrel of cold water adjoins the communal hot tub. From time to time a soaker douses his pinkened body in it, and emerges exhilarated. A cold water hose nearby will accomplish nearly the same thing. Claims are made that hot-cold alterations are great for skin tone.

It's pleasant to enclose the tub area in arbors and trellises. Flowering vines such as honeysuckle, jasmine and cereus will ingratiate the air. Also consider installing a small speaker to a nearby tree or wall.

40

HEALTH

Physicians confirm what we already know—hot tub soaking is beneficial. It relaxes muscles, dilates blood vessels and helps circulation. Buoyancy helps venous return. Soaking is good for people with heart trouble, varicose veins and high blood pressure. Older people who have suffered previous strokes, however, should be cautioned against soaking alone. Those with hardening of the arteries should abstain. Contrary to common belief, a hot bath does not help to dissipate a fever. Nor is it a cure for intoxication. Otherwise, a hot tub soak is heartily recommended for whatever ails you.

PSYCHIATRIC ASPECTS

Psychiatric authorities such as Rollo May have characterized our era as schizoid. In an increasingly crowded world we are constantly thrown together, yet we feel a growing sense of isolation and estrangement from each other. People crave closeness, yet find themselves unable to achieve it.

Various people have sought solutions to this problem in communal living. Another solution is the communal hot tub. Tubs provide the closeness that everyone craves. The very nature of the hot tub experience—a small group soaking together nude in a heated tub—provides a sense of warmth and community.

"The small hot tub might be considered a womblike milieu especially conducive to relaxation and openness. The nudity might well express an attitude which could be an antidote to the often frustrating attempts to achieve intimacy through mechanical sexuality. It could also promote a healthy atmosphere in which one could overcome shyness or oversensitivity about body image or fear of exposure.

"In summary, I believe the communal hot tub represents a very sane approach towards overcoming the schizoid trends in our society by providing a relaxed and meaningful intimacy."—*H. Neil Karp, M.D.*

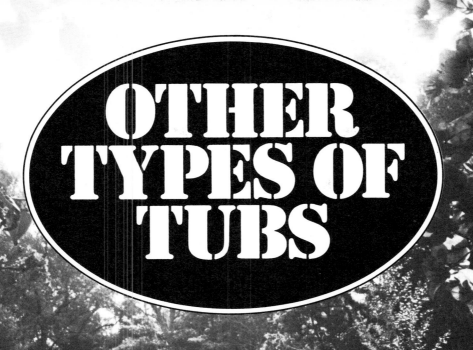

OTHER TYPES OF TUBS

THE CANNIBAL POT

The simplest, and in some ways the best, answer to the mechanics in hot tubbery was conceived and executed by Santa Barbara county supervisor Frank Frost. His tub (above) resembles a giant concrete soup bowl, stuccoed on the outside and ringed by inlaid tile. In the bottom Frost inserted a thick iron plate which conducts heat from a simple gas burner that slides underneath. The water is heated directly, with no need for pumps, plumbing or elaborate heaters. When the water reaches the desired temperature Frost, like an alert chef, simply turns off the gas. His guests call it the cannibal pot, and some have been known to become apprehensive when he appears at tubside with onions and carrots. Here are Frost's construction diagrams:

46

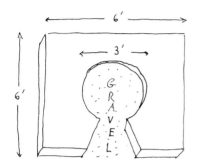

Make a concrete foundation 4 inches high. Dig out the middle a foot deep and fill with gravel. This is for drainage during rain or overflows.

Get a one-fourth-inch steel plate 3+ feet square. Weld reinforcing rods to it as shown after bending rods into shape. (Your ironmonger will weld for you.)

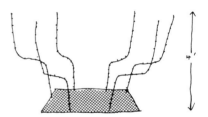

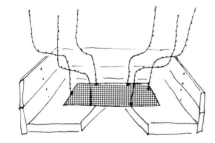

Put the plate over the "keyhole." Build forms out of old two-by-tens. You are going to have concrete poured to cover the horizontal bend in the rods.

To form up the center depression take cardboard cartons, cut them up and tape them to make a cylinder. Then fill the cylinder with tightly packed dirt. The concrete man will giggle, but it works.

Don't forget a drain pipe.

Now have concrete poured, or rent a small mixer and do it yourself. Order about two yards—and make the forms *strong!*

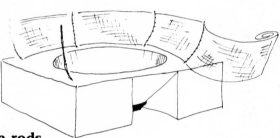

Wait a week, then remove the forms. Wrap the rods with two layers of wire mesh, one-fourth inch on the outside, larger on the inside.

Paint with swimming pool paint.

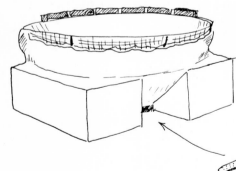

Build up the sides by hand, patty-cake fashion, using a mortar mix, 4 to 1 sand to cement. Top off with some nice Mexican bricks. Run a gas line out and connect a burner with some flexible gas hose; it heats about six to seven degrees per hour.

THE GREENHOUSE POOL

In the oaks behind their stone house, Jon and Zig Knoll had a sturdy old glass greenhouse, long neglected. Zig is a belly dancer and poet, Jon a research engineer. Their interest was in growing edible things like avocados, oranges, apricots and vegetables, making exotic wines, raising worms and grinding compost rather than raising orchids. They had a mutual need to soak away the tensions of their busy lives. So one fine day, with sledge and pick they attacked the concrete greenhouse floor and bashed through a five-foot circle. Then they dug. A few weekends later they had themselves a sunken hot pool of reinforced concrete and a neat system of pipes and valves, perfectly planned and executed. A fountain pump circulates water between a twenty-gallon tank heater and the pool or, by a turning of valves, pumps it out into the orchard through a hose. The pool provides an ideal climate for a huge, looming staghorn fern and friends in need.

49

THE BOULDERED POOL

The most idyllic tub, where man's handiwork is nearly invisible, is John Smith's bouldered pool. The bottom of his land extends through an oak grove, an ancient waterway where room-sized boulders were casually tossed. Here, on a narrow plateau that parallels the present-day creek, Smith found a perfect nest of boulders. He excavated a few yards of leaf mold, hid buried boulders and mortared the seams, troweling in a fairly smooth bottom. When it was filled with hot water no one would suspect that this sublime pool wasn't a natural hot spring. Since it is a great distance from a gas line, Smith must lug in a couple of portable butane tanks to fuel his heater which stands like a sentry alongside the pool. The only real drawback to a bouldered tub is that in the beginning the stones soak up much heat. But once they have done their absorbing, they tend to keep the water warm. Walking down the trail through a sloping avocado orchard, winding through an oak grove, parting the final branches to see revealed this steaming pool—this is a visit to Eden.

THE PLYWOOD TUB

In striking contrast to the natural bouldered pool is the sunken plywood tub Vic Kondra found in the backyard of a house he bought in a conventional neighborhood. Like a swimming pool, it is surrounded by decking, fencing on two sides, and an arbor. The previous owner, Don Timm, had given a summer of ambition and energy to build his personal spa. He began by digging a rectangular hole six by eight feet, three feet deep. He lined it with three-quarter-inch marine plywood which he glassed on both sides. Then he built in a pair of benches running the long way, one sixteen inches high for short people (their children), and the other twelve inches high for grownups. Timm's wife, with talents as a muralist, painted the inner walls with sweeping aquarian designs. Kondra likes his water hotter than any Westerner we know—a piping 120 degrees. With a super "Aldheet" 420,000 Btu. flash heater, he heats a thousand gallons of cold water in less than an hour and a half.

THE CUDDLE TUB

In Isla Vista, adjoining the campus of the University of California at Santa Barbara, is a road called El Nido (The Nest) where there is a grove of tall Island pines. In one of the pines there is a gigantic crow's-nest which is actually a house where a boatbuilder lives. At the foot of the tree is another kind of nest—a water nest. It is Richard Peterson's cuddle tub, barely 24 inches square and 27 inches high. Unbelievably, it holds two people—if they are compatible. It's a simple box made of two-by-tens, doweled, pegged, glued and then glassed with resin. A regular sink drain was installed in the bottom. Hot water is piped over from the water heater of a nearby house. "We even got a third nestled in here one night," Peterson said, "but don't ask me how."

THE YIN-YANG POOLS

Carved into the cliffs above the ocean is a pair of interlocking spiraled pools on a tiled terrace below the house of Eric Cassirer. A 3 h.p. industrial pump pushing water through a four-inch main at the rate of four hundred gallons per minute gives the water motion and activates a series of two-inch jet streams. The first is aimed at your feet, and as you follow the curve into deeper water, others play upon your knees, waist and shoulders. Cassirer designed and plumbed these hot pools after studying the spas of Europe. Adjoining the pools he built a cold, cascading waterfall. Directly behind is a bathhouse with a sauna and a massage room.

On this part of the coast, the ocean is to the south. The pools are oriented so you can lie in the shallows, your head to the north, and watch passing ships and whales. You are in the attitude of a compass needle, a clue to the further meaning that Cassirer gives his facility—*vitron energy awareness.* At the very edge of the cliff he had welded a steel tripod tower which he claims serves as an energy antenna. Its base encloses a tubful of magnetite sand over which hangs a magnet. This tower is tied into the steel webbing embedded in the pools' concrete, and into the reinforcing rods of the stone walls. The stones themselves were selected for their energy potential and trucked in from Mexico. All this is to implement Cassirer's own massage techniques designed to draw energy up from the legs through body blocks and thus to sensitize the whole person.

It is inspiring enough to lie in this pool on the cliff on the edge of the Western world, feel the sea breeze across your face and gaze at the breathing ocean.

PLUG
YOUR TUB INTO
THE SUN

The first solar-heated hot tub in Santa Barbara was installed by the ever-resourceful Fred Carr. This was a particularly challenging job because the family he built it for had an 800-gallon tub and lived in the foothills beyond the range of natural gas. In addition, propane was rationed, and an electric pool heater would have been beyond their means. Heretofore, solar heating had been used only to supplement conventional heaters. Now the challenge was to devise a system that would bring water to hot-tubbing temperatures and rely exclusively on solar heat. The potential existed—the south coast climate is benevolent and an existing roof was just begging to be helpful.

Before Carr could design a proper system, he researched the available solar absorbers on the market. There is indeed nothing new under the sun, and solar heating has been researched and experimented with for years throughout the world. The French, for example, had devised optic systems—parabolic lenses on power mounts that tracked the sun. Sophisticated solar cells had been developed for Skylab. Naturally, these Buck Rogers-ish concepts didn't apply to the problem on hand, which called for a small expenditure of money. For a million dollars, I'm sure Carr could have come up with something—say a giant magnifying glass that would have had eight hundred gallons of water sizzling in a matter of seconds.

So Carr pored through all the solar heating plans and spec sheets he could find. If the world's technology had been developing solar absorbers for years, there was no need to start from scratch. "Why reinvent the wheel?" he asked. Most existing absorbers, he discovered, utilized copper or polyethylene tubing, and these he rejected as inefficient. Water flowing smoothly through a round tube absorbs heat only on its upper circumference; the bottom half of the tube is hidden from direct rays of the sun. Furthermore, mineral deposits from the water will eventually crust the walls of the tube and make matters even worse. Carr also rejected those absorbers designed for a "greenhouse effect" and covered by sheets of glass. They would work efficiently only when the sun was directly overhead; slanting rays would be reflected off. Not everyone lives on the equator.

The design that excited him, the *Solarator,* comes in 36-by-74-inch panels of a black matt absorptive plastic. It is a "sandwich," the interior a labyrinth of flattened PVC tubing with turbulators that tumble the water, giving it maximum

contact with the heating surface and increasing heating efficiency. Temperatures exceeding 150° have been recorded under experimental conditions. These panels are manufactured in Michigan and distributed on the West Coast by Solar Systems Sales in Novato, California.

Carr had high hopes for this "roundest wheel" of all. He reckoned that four panels would do the job for the 800-gallon tub. They cost less than fifty dollars each and would easily pay for themselves in a year by fuel saved.

Adjoining the hot tub was a studio with a flat roof, thirteen feet above tub level. Carr calculated that a 1/12 h.p. centrifugal pump would circulate the water adequately. In selecting a pump, the features to consider are head, lift and volume. A Grainger's pump catalog or your local pump distributor can help you there. For this project, a pump was needed to deliver four gallons a minute to feed four panels at a thirteen-foot elevation. (Carr measured the flow with a graduated bucket and a sweep second hand.) A centrifugal pump is quieter and lives longer than a gear-type pump.

Before building a frame for the panels, Carr laid down a layer of mirrored (silver) mylar on the flat roof. Sheets of flat aluminum would be more durable, but would cost more. This reflective backing bounces heat back to the absorbers, heat that otherwise might get away.

The panel frame was built of two-by-fours and plywood. To get maximum direct sun, add ten degrees to your latitude in winter and subtract ten degrees in summer. Since Santa Barbara is at thirty-five degrees, Carr's frames were sloped at forty-five degrees, facing due south. Use a compass. (In the Southern Hemisphere, of course, face them north.)

The panels come with inlet and outlet hose fittings. They are easily installed using a screwdriver, pliers and a pocket knife. They should be connected in parallel, not in series, to avoid radiation loss and high pressure; each panel has one gallon of water per minute passing through it. The panels were fastened to the frame along the top with brass staples, the bottoms and sides left free to draw up when water was pumped through. The system was plumbed with black agricultural tubing, although ¾-inch garden hose will work also. The tubing is cheaper and its blackness helps absorb a wee bit more heat.

As you can see from the accompanying diagram, the solar heating system is independent from the filtering system. You may wonder why the need for a

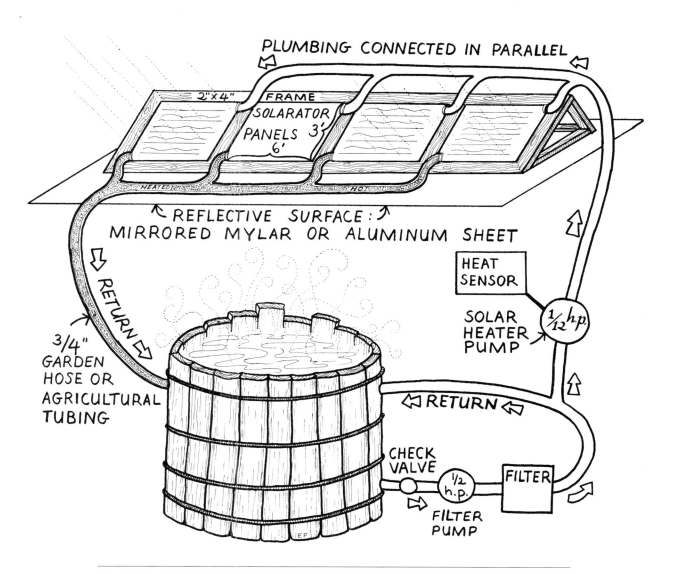

PLUMBING CONNECTED IN PARALLEL

2"x4" FRAME
SOLARATOR PANELS 3'
6'

HEATED   HOT

REFLECTIVE SURFACE:
MIRRORED MYLAR OR ALUMINUM SHEET

RETURN

3/4"
GARDEN
HOSE OR
AGRICULTURAL
TUBING

HEAT
SENSOR

SOLAR
HEATER
PUMP

1/12 h.p.

RETURN

CHECK
VALVE

1/2
h.p.

FILTER

FILTER
PUMP

SCHEMATIC DIAGRAM OF "SOLARATOR" HEATER

second pump. The filter pump needs a half horsepower to push water through the filtering membranes, while a mere one-twelfth horsepower is all the solar system needs. The difference in power consumption is like comparing the power used by a Christmas tree bulb to that used by a heat lamp.

Carr devised a heat sensor—a glass-topped black aluminum box containing an attic fan thermostat set at ninety degrees. This was wired to the solar pump like a switch. The system would then turn on with the sun, draw water from the filter line, push it up through the solar absorbers, and return it through a separate line to the tub.

One small problem remained—how to cope with a prevailing ocean breeze that came up-canyon and robbed heat from the panels? One solution was to box the panels in glass, but this not only was expensive, but also would reflect some heat away by slanting the rays, as mentioned earlier. The best solution, Carr determined, was to create a pressure cushion by boxing in the perimeter of each panel with a one-by-twelve. This created a favorable aerodynamic situation: the breeze bounced off the sides and passed over the top of the box without intruding upon the trapped cushion of hot air above each panel.

That accomplished, the first Santa Barbara solar-heated hot tub was in operation—piping hot from a day's sun. Kept covered when not in use, the stout redwood walls held in the heat through a June night with less than five degrees loss. Needless to say, when it's stormy or foggy, forget it—unless you want to supplement solar heating with a fuel heater.

An English friend threw up his hands at the seeming complexity of this system and wondered why a simple slanting wall of black corrugated aluminum with a gutter on the bottom and a fine spray hose stretched across the top wouldn't do as well. It would do, but not nearly as well. Water and heat loss by evaporation would be excessive, and the poor pump would be working overtime to compensate. Covering the wall with glass to prevent evaporation would only create the disadvantages cited previously.

From available technology, Carr's system is indeed superior to any other we know, unless you want to consider a $10,000 pivoting lens or an actual pipeline to the sun.

A SMOKELESS (BUT STEAMY) INDUSTRY IS BORN

Fred Carr was perched on the edge of his hot tub with sawdust in his beard, picking at a nagging splinter in his thumb. It was midsummer '73 and a dozen of his friends were soaking or lounging in the Sunday-afternoon sun. "There must be an easier way," Carr said with a wince. "Finished putting in Ken's tub this morning. The staves are crusty with cream of tartar crystals, and it's no fun trying to grind them off. If we try dissolving them with soda ash, it could take weeks."

His friends commiserated. A month ago Carr had bought up twenty old wine vats from a bankrupt winery and sold them at cost to friends, figuring they were handy enough with tools to put them together themselves. He had even xeroxed instructions that made it seem simple. Yet there were certain subtleties in coopering that were second nature to Carr, but confounding to most others. So in the end he had to come to the rescue and reconstruct the tubs for them. To compound problems, many of the old vats had warped or split staves, were coated with tartar crystals (a natural by-product of aging wine), or needed to be cut down in height. On top of that, many of his friends had acquired old heaters, cranky pumps and obsolete filters that needed resurrecting. Like a country doctor, Carr found himself rushing from one patient to another during that hectic month.

His wife consoled him with a back rub. "The easier way would be to forget the junkyards. They serve their purpose for folks who live off the land and who are clever enough to do their own jerry-rigging, and lucky enough to find an old tank somewhere. I've got another twenty people clamoring for hot tubs, and the only answer is to work with new equipment. Having learned the hard way, it'll be easy to design an efficient system that would go together quickly and do its job well." He called across the tub to Ken Palmer: "Hey, if you're not busy this afternoon, let's start a company!"

They named it The Original Santa Barbara Hotub Company. By marketing a complete hot tub system, ready to go, Carr and Palmer lifted hot tubism from the esoteric realm of western foothill people to the whole populace of America. It meant that anyone anywhere could, for a sum, have a hot tub delivered to his backyard and a day later could be soaking away crystals of Old Thought. An adventurous idea. People live in colonies and tend to regard outsiders as alien. But naked, without the status indicators of daily costuming, whether it be Funk-

and-Flash or Wall-Street-Gray, they find themselves in a universal league. Then too, there's the awareness of nature by immersing in it. Food is better outdoors; so is soaking.

It took eight months to make the company work. Carr and Palmer accepted a third partner, Ray Fraker, who owned a pool supply company and knew some of the secrets of hydrodynamics and heat exchange and also knew sources of supply for all the plumbing elements. They put their heads together, erected an experimental hot tub system and spent some weeks tinkering, revising, and simplifying until they evolved a palletized support equipment package to their satisfaction. They also contracted with a long-established cooperage in the redwood country of northern California to custom-mill tubs in three sizes to their specifications.

They rented a shed in Carpinteria, on the outskirts of Santa Barbara, set up power tools, devised jigs and quickly achieved the capability of assembling and shipping a thousand hot tubs a year. The first orders were local; then they began coming in from up and down the West Coast. One day an order drifted in from Houston; the next week, from Nova Scotia and Vermont. Inquiries poured in from everywhere. Long-distance calls. Obviously, the appeal of hot tubs reached far beyond the original coterie of foothill enthusiasts. Some of the Mountain Drive originators grumbled and felt that proliferation was profane. They were losing their exclusivity. But isn't that what Understanding is all about?

Early in '74 two men from Los Angeles drove north in their Mercedes to visit the hot tub gang. They had never seen one in the flesh before, much less been in one. They were dapper men; one wore a three-button suit and a striped tie. They looked out of place in the grungy shed. They said they wanted to talk business.

"There's only one place for that," Fred replied, wiping beer suds from his beard. He climbed into his clanking flatbed truck and guided them to his canyon house. His wife served herb tea while they waited for Palmer and Fraker to appear. The men introduced themselves as Larry Resnick and Bob Lagunoff, representing an investor's group interested in marketing hot tubs world-wide. "We'll have to discuss that in an appropriate setting," Fred declared. He led them outside to his oval tub, undressed, hosed off the day's dust and lowered himself into the water. Palmer and Fraker arrived with bottles of wine and sunk in too. After some hesitation, the men from Los Angeles got in, draping their clothes carefully over the stub of a woodpeckered telephone pole.

Carr laughed. "I can't get over it—you guys coming up here to talk hot tubs when you could be dealing with condominiums and bonds."

"We've had enough of that," Resnick sighed, wiping steam from his glasses. "We're here because the idea intrigues us, not as a moneymaker alone, but because it really sounds like a lovable product."

They seemed strange tubfellows at first, but the lull of the water, the paternalism of the oak and the benevolence of the redwood melted away their differences.

From this first discussion, a marketing company was formed. Resnick and Lagunoff set up retail dealerships and instituted an export program. By summer, hot tubs had outgrown their western provincialism and had gained recognition across the country, as well as overseas.

This isn't meant to be the biography of a company, but simply evidence of the hot tub's wide appeal. While this book opens with guidelines for the do-it-yourselfer who is willing to scrounge and improvise with minimal cash outlay, it ends with a description of the luxurious Hotub and its preplumbed support system that sells, erected on your site, for approximately $2,500. You may gulp at the figure, yet it is half the cost of the average fiberglass or concrete spas, and operating costs are one-third. If you have the money and don't have the time or inclination to do it yourself, this is the best answer.

ANATOMY OF THE HOTUB

REDWOOD TUB

Milled entirely from kiln-dried, clear heart northern California redwood. Staves and floor planks are from two-inch stock, allow little heat loss and will last a lifetime. Iron hoops are 1/2 inch thick, far superior to bands.

PUMP

Water is pulled from the tub at the rate of sixty gallons a minute through a 1-1/2-inch heat-retaining, noncorrosive PVC suction line and enters the pump through a strainer pot that removes hair, leaves and lint. The pump has a bronze housing that won't warp as plastic will, or rust as cast iron does. Its seal design eliminates high-speed vibration which normally impairs motor efficiency and life. The pump is driven by a 1/2 h.p., thermo-protected motor that can run on 110 or 220 volts. Its bearings are sealed and need no oiling.

TUBMASTER FILTER

Unlike earlier filters that purify water with diatomaceous earth or sand, which must be backwashed and refilled frequently, the Tubmaster filter consists of nine accordioned polyester modules that strain out foreign matter, oils and lotions. These units snap out by hand and are cleaned by washing in a simple solution of tri-sodium phosphate. A pressure gauge tells you when it's time to clean them— usually two or three times a year.

HEATER

A gas-fired 70,000 Btu. glass-lined tank with a thermostat that permits a maximum tub water temperature of 112 degrees. The thermostat can be set at any temperature below this.

The company also offers optional equipment such as "Tub-Fingers" and "Tub Vigor," hydromassage air injection accessories for those who aren't content with the tranquility of still water, and an array of conveniences such as underwater benches, shelves, skimmers and herbal sachets. The Original Santa Barbara Hotub Company can be reached at 41 Mountain Drive, Santa Barbara, California 93013.

By the time this book gets in the stores, other hot tub makers may have sprung up. The time has come, people are ready. Hot tubs are becoming a part of the life style of the seventies.

HOTUB KIT INCLUDES:

staves (milled, beveled and grooved)
1 stave with thru-wall fittings installed
bottom boards (shaped and predrilled for dowels)
dowels (cut to length)
chime joists (cut to size)
heavy rod hoops (rounded and threaded)
lugs and nuts
1 can of mastic

TOOLS AND MATERIALS REQUIRED (NOT FURNISHED):

1 friend	1 putty knife
1 small sledge hammer	1 handful of small 1-1/2″ nails
1 10″ crescent wrench	3 pieces of lath
1 level	

GENERAL INFORMATION

This HOTUB is milled from clear heart redwood. The average person, with a helper, should be able to assemble it in less than three hours. The entire weight of the filled tub is borne by the bottom boards, not the staves. The load is transferred to the foundation by means of the chime joists. If you have firm level ground or a concrete or brick paved area, concrete foundation piers should not be necessary. Good drainage is important, however. The chime joists provide a minimum of 2 inches of clearance below the staves to allow for free circulation of air. No dirt or backfill material should come in contact with the tub. The HOTUB, when filled for the first time, may leak slightly. This is normal. Like a wooden boat, the wet wood will swell and become watertight within a day or so.

HOTUBS & SEX

BY GEORGE BERONIUS

It struck me as a frankly intriguing idea to observe the hot tub cultists at close range and report the impact of the phenomenon on marriage and morals. But caveat emptor—I caution against drawing quick conclusions from what I report. It comes to me that social custom is very similar to the unadorned human form: it can be totally different things to different people.

Most of the male hot tubbers I interviewed insist that sex is not a part of it. However, have you ever met a male who admitted sex was hidden inside a box of candy? Or under the foliage of a dozen red roses? Or in that initial dry martini? One wild-eyed fellow did blurt out that the whole custom was no more than a good way to render women naked and defenseless. And while it is true that some men are probably more curious about women's naked bodies than about anything else in life, a full-fledged conspiracy hardly seems likely.

But if sex isn't in it somewhere, why all the fuss? Why should nude bathing have so much appeal to so many?

I raised the question first with an especially articulate tub devotee, a former newspaper reporter who is now an esteemed public-relations counselor. "Face it," he said, "the hot tub is no panacea. Its sexual implications have been vastly overdrawn.

"For some," he continued, "the nude communal bath is purely social. For others, it is therapeutic. In our family it replaces pillow talk."

"But doesn't that bring us right back to sex?" I inquired.

"Perhaps I should clear up something for you," he said, looking at me directly and smiling tolerantly. "One half-hour in 110-degree water results without exception in what might best be described as the 'boiled-noodle effect.'"

It seemed unnecessary to pursue that aspect of the subject further, so we went back to discussing the psychology of it. How, I asked, do married couples adjust to sitting around naked in mixed doubles?

"Well, I suppose some do go in for being unaccused Peeping Toms," the counselor ventured. "Sure, boys like to look at girls. But"—and here he

winked—"it has been my observation that most of us look much better with clothes on. I think you quickly get over that sort of thing. It's what you bring to the tub, not what comes out of it."

Next I called on a (male) psychologist who writes books on child behavior and, as I ascertained from glancing around his house, evidently dabbles in nude photography. "But of course it is sexually motivated," he laughed, brushing aside all my spirit-of-community stuff.

"There is inevitable sexual excitement in any change from a condition of less exposure and less physical closeness to greater exposure and greater closeness."

I asked if he felt communal nudity was in some way necessary to modern marriage. "Oh sure, sure," he replied. "Same as any other pleasurable or social relationship."

"What about the dangers?"

"There are dangers in all social relationships," he responded.

Then I told him about the boiled-noodle effect.

"Ah, yes. That can be a certain deterrent," he said, nodding sagely.

It began to strike me that what I was lacking in this interview was the viewpoint of a woman. The wife of one enthusiastic hot tubber declined to be interviewed at all. She was a member of a very prominent San Francisco family and feared being discovered. But finally I discovered Callista McAllister among Leon Elder's acquaintances.

"Having sat, floated or floundered in countless hot tubs with friends of both sexes," Ms. McAllister admitted, "I divine that women feel differently about bare groups than men do."

How so, I asked?

"Bare men don't admire each other. Bare women do."

One thing you hear a lot about from the cultists is the restorative powers of the hot tub: "Owning a hot tub is like adding a room onto your life." But what about that vaunted spirit of community? Would one necessarily feel better about buying a used car from a salesman one had met in a hot tub? Would one be less wary about starting a friendship with a member of the opposite sex one had met while soaking? I pondered this, and I still do. Hot tubs, like human bodies, say different things to different people.

AFTERWORD & FOREWARNING

If you do go ahead and build your own hot tub you'll find it's like adding a room to your life—if not a new dimension. You soon learn that while few bodies are classically beautiful, none are ugly. To compare the fat to the lithe is like juxtaposing a Lachaise to a Giacometti. You soak with infants, grandparents and all ages in between, and learn there are neither terrible secrets nor mysteries of the universe to be seen. Secrets and mysteries are as elusive as ever, but you gain a *quality* of camaraderie that is unique.

Your life expands, but so do your chores. It's one thing to get the tub ready—the filling and heating, trimming the candles, folding up towels and laying a fire for the *après* bath—that's only half of it. The dirty work comes the morning after as you discover soggy footprints have tracked up your house, the empty beer cans and little hills of dirty towels, anonymous garments and the murkiness of the tub itself. Whatever happened to that sparkling water that surged from the hose? You forgot to put the lid on at bedtime and now dead leaves are coasting on the surface. Some have become waterlogged and have sunk to join a maroon sock on the bottom. You reach for it and yelp—the water is a scalding 140 degrees because you forgot to turn off the heater.

You groan as you remember last night's crisis. You had invited Bill and Mary Newcomer over, little suspecting they were having marital problems. At hot tub time Mary had gaily stripped with the others and romped down to the tub. Bill preferred to fume and pace the house. Now and then he'd stomp out on the porch and yell down at the tub, "Big deal!" He refused to go in himself or give her reprieve. Ugly, but it happens sometimes, making you, the host, feel somehow responsible, though you know you're not.

You screw a long hose onto the drain valve and pull it down the slope with you to the new trees. As the tub water fills the basin of a young avocado you think of the nourishment it's getting, more than plain water would give. You had eleven happy people over last night, and one grump. The grump didn't get in, so really what you are doing now is giving happy water to your tree.

Later, after you've given the tub its scrubdown and you gaze at the new water filling it, you catch yourself humming with expectation. You turn on the pump and heater eagerly. It's then you realize you've become a tub freak.

My father got it
some where—he
used to be a missionary.

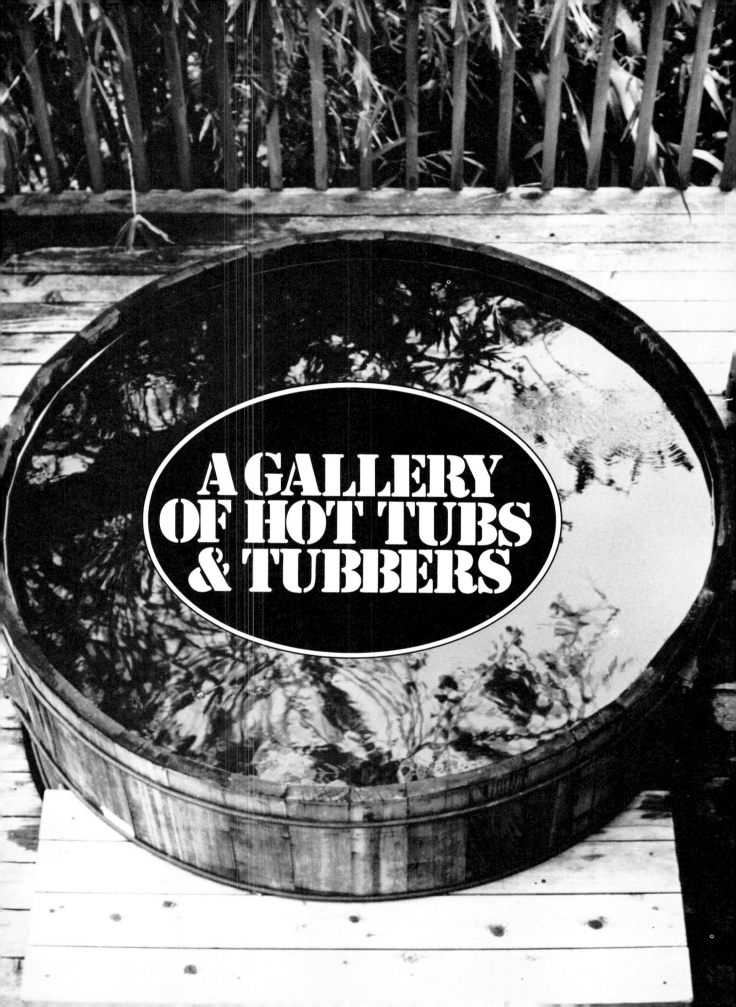

A GALLERY
OF HOT TUBS
& TUBBERS

I first saw and felt a classical Japanese *ofuro* in Kokura while on R and R from the Korean War. The luxury of being enveloped by 110-degree water was matched only by the companionship; there I was, a timid American, huddled in my corner while whole smiling Japanese families filed in and out of the huge communal vat, exclaiming with delight to one another as the molten liquid dissolved their sinews. At that time I vowed I would someday have my own party-sized tub, thinking that such an appliance would be unique in America.

It was only a few years later that I moved to Santa Barbara and found that there were indeed hot tubs in America and that most of them were in Santa Barbara. I had been in many of the town's tubs when, years later, it was finally possible for me to build my own, and I am no less pleasured by a tub and good fellowship now than I was my first time twenty-five years ago in Kokura.

So far as I know, Santa Barbara remains the hot tub capital of America, and as a public official of that part of Santa Barbara County where hot tubism was born, I invite readers of all origins, creeds, cults and karasses to investigate this aspect of our indigenous culture, to be inspired and to help spread this most civilized of customs through a deserving world. —*Santa Barbara County Supervisor Frank J. Frost*

Soaking is not a body concert. Those who have tubs are not entertaining orgies. The familiarity of the tub is essential, not sexual. Being a belly dancer I easily testify to the healing power of the tub. Aches and pains disappear in the water. Two hours of dancing to an hour's soaking. Our hot tub is a great fluid mother who soothes our anxieties while we warm in her belly.—*Zig Knoll*

In far-off lands and times gone by, each man knew his place and function. When to bow first, when second. Where to command, where to obey. Who to touch, who to shun. Everyone had his own village, tribe or lodge, his own religion, caste or class. The family bulged with grandparents, uncles, cousins, aunts and hangers-on. Each person was secure in his own group, understood by all according to his role.

Now we drift on a vast, heaving plane littered with campers and trailers, strewn with abandoned careers, suburban bedrooms, broken homes, planned slums, transferred employees and fortified condominia. Everyone is our neighbor, but no one is our friend. Surviving grandparents have defected to retirement colonies. Childhood chums are scattered by the winds of opportunity. Our living quarters are too small, our schedules too tight or our standards too strict to accommodate visiting clansmen. Hemmed in on all sides, we feel bereft and alone.

The hot tub temporarily shuts out this unsatisfying world and restores our sense of community. Bathed in its comforting warmth, we ritually reenact our common origin. Instant amniotic comrades, we need no roles to play, but gaze contentedly into one another's faces, wondering where the boundary between one person and another lies, or if there is a boundary. Born again into the cold night air, we find ourselves once more discrete individuals, but no longer isolated, as the memory of that brief, unspoken coalescence lingers and glows.—*Richard de Mille*

HAVING SAT,
FLOATED OR
FLOUNDERED
IN COUNTLESS
HOT TUBS WITH
FRIENDS OF
ALL SEXES,

I divine that women feel differently about bare groups than men do. It may go all the way back to the baboon or to the abominable screwman, but I think we must admit that men are sexually more aggressive than women are. Bare men don't admire each other much. Bare women may admire each other, or may pretend to if they feel bitchy . . . At any rate, all this discord and uptightness gets washed away by hot water. Sink into the tub, and you'll begin to shed the dead skin of your previous persona and find a smoother one underneath. It happens when you sit around with naked friends and neighbors for a few hours. Suddenly you realize you are looking at persons instead of bodies. The bareness just makes you feel that each person is easier to get to. This accessibility can be an illusion, of course. The man or woman who can't give out any tenderness or expose any vulnerability with clothes on probably can't learn to do it with clothes off either. But often it is real.

You have to start with people you can trust, people who respect you, people who can take you the way you are, people who find you trustworthy, respectful and accepting, too. A tall order! But then you can find yourself facing a sweet, open soul, whose undefended body keeps whispering, "Here I am. Look at me. Take me. I'm yours. I'm not holding anything back." And you realize that you love that person. Next time you meet, you put your arms around each other and say, "Remember when we were in the womb together?" And he or she says, "Yes, yes," and squeezes you and sighs a big sigh, and it is hardly erotic at all, but it is lovely.—*Callista McAllister*

Santa Barbara must be the world center for the hot tub as described in this book. Santa Barbara has almost a utopian climate; it never gets very cold or very hot, and evenings when hot bathing is at its best are often blessed with warm gentle breezes coming off the Santa Ynez mountains, and these airs are laden with the scent of blooming pittosporum or jasmine, and if the flowers fail a drop of patchouli oil in the water is very nice.

Some say, "Solitary bathing is a sin." And truly, once one has experienced the languid delight, the magnificent sociability and the beauty of the invigorating aftermath of the outdoor hot tub, one tends to agree. A hot tub gathering shouldn't be considered as a lewd bacchanal. I prefer to think of a hot bath as a beautiful orgy *without* sex. I recommend it heartily. Solitary bathing *is* a sin. — *Dick Johnston*

ELDER BY CHRISTIANS

DABNEY BY CRAWFORD

CRAWFORD BY DABNEY

MCCALL BY MCCALL

MACDOUGALL by MACDOUGALL

Other Hot Tub Makers

Santa Barbara Hotub Co.
41 Mountain Drive
Santa Barbara
California
93103

Sausalito Hot Tub Company
Sausalito
California
94965

Clive Scullion
Berkeley
California
94904

The Splinter Group
Oakland
California
94904

California Hot Tub Company
232 Glenwood Avenue
Woodside
California
94062